Math Masters

Operations and Algebraic Thinking

Running for Class President

Represent and Solve Problems Involving Division

Richelle Jackson

PowerKiDS press™

NEW YORK

Published in 2015 by The Rosen Publishing Group, Inc.
29 East 21st Street, New York, NY 10010

Book Design: Katelyn Londino

Photo Credits: Cover, p. 9 (background) Chris Clinton/The Image Bank/Getty Images; pp. 3–24 (background) blue67design/Shutterstock.com; p. 5 Monkey Business Images/Shutterstock.com; p. 7 Jamie Grill/The Image Bank/Getty Images; p. 9 (kids holding poster) Sergey Novikov/Shutterstock.com; p. 11 Brand X Pictures/Thinkstock.com; p. 13 Rob Byron/Shutterstock.com; p. 15 Chris Clinton/Taxi/Getty Images; p. 17 (desk) Reinhold Leitner/Shutterstock.com; p. 17 (button) Steve Wood/Shutterstock.com; p. 19 Andersen Ross/Blend Images/Getty Images; p. 21 Jupiterimages/Thinkstock.com; p. 22 Andresr/Shutterstock.com.

Library of Congress Cataloging-in-Publication Data

Jackson, Richelle, author.
 Running for class president : represent and solve problems involving division / Richelle Jackson.
    pages cm. — (Math masters. Operations and algebraic thinking)
 Includes index.
ISBN 978-1-4777-4959-3 (pbk.)
ISBN 978-1-4777-4960-9 (6-pack)
ISBN 978-1-4777-6448-0 (library binding)
1. Division—Juvenile literature. 2. Mathematics—Juvenile literature. 3. School elections—Juvenile literature. I. Title.
QA115.J33 2015
513.2′14—dc23
                          2014000219

Manufactured in the United States of America

CPSIA Compliance Information: Batch #WS15RC: For further information contact Rosen Publishing, New York, New York at 1-800-237-9932.

3195 3522

Contents

Back to School

Summer vacation just ended. It's time to start a new year of school. We hold an election for class president at the beginning of every school year. The students in my class get to vote for the person we think would be the best president.

What is the class president's job? He or she thinks of fun activities for our class to do, like raising money for field trips. Our class president also **represents** our class in meetings with the presidents of other classes.

Being the class president is a lot of responsibility. You have to be fair and willing to work hard.

This year's election is going to be very exciting. That's because I've decided to run for president of my class! I have a lot of good ideas and plans that I think will make my classmates want to elect me. I know I would do a good job.

Before the election takes place, I have to **campaign** to be elected. Campaigning is everything you do to tell people why they should vote for you.

I want to run for class president because
I think I can do a good job leading the class.

Vote for Molly

Lopez for President

Election Today!

Running My Campaign

Campaigning is a lot of work. I have to make posters and give a speech in front of the whole class. Sometimes, people hand out **flyers** or small prizes with their name on them as part of their campaign. This may make people want to vote for them.

My friends are going to help me campaign. I'm **dividing** the work that needs to be done. If everyone does a little bit, the work will get done much faster.

To divide means you split something up into equal shares. You can think of dividing as how many times a small number can go into a larger number.

Election Posters

I work on my campaign during the weekend before the election. I have 4 of my friends over to make posters. My mom bought 50 pieces of poster paper. If we all make the same number of posters, how many will each of us make? Dividing 50 posters by 5 people means we'll each make 10.

I have 10 colored pencils to use when we make posters. How many colored pencils will each of us have if I divide them evenly?

To do these equations, or math problems, divide the total number of objects by the number of people who will use them. So, dividing 10 colored pencils by 5 people means we each get 2 colored pencils.

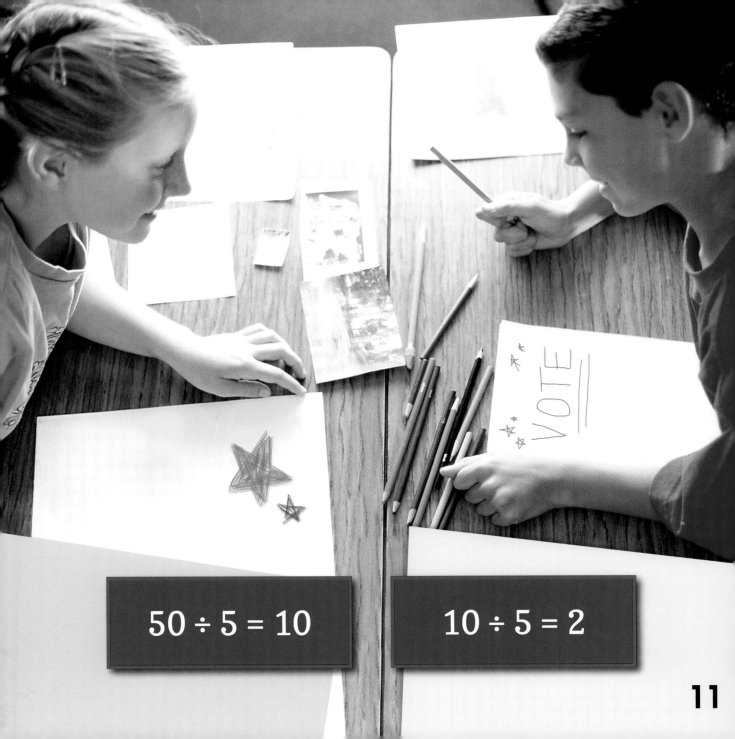

$$50 \div 5 = 10$$

$$10 \div 5 = 2$$

I bring my posters to class on Monday. My teacher says I can hang them up around my school. I hang 5 posters in my classroom and the hallway near my class. I have 45 left to hang. Some of my friends are going to hang the rest for me.

I have 9 friends who want to help hang my posters. How many posters should each friend get? I can use a question mark to stand for the missing number.

For this equation, I know the dividend (45) and the quotient (9). I need to find the divisor. I know the missing number is 5.

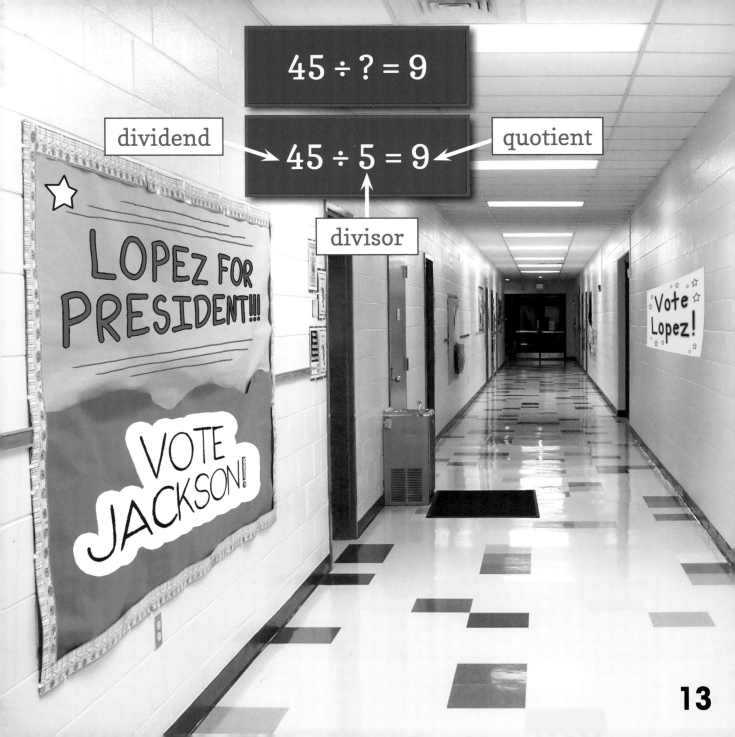

Flyers, Buttons, and Pencils

I think handing out flyers will help me win the class election. I print 80. I have 4 days to hand them out. If I divide 80 flyers by 4 days, I'll hand out 20 flyers a day.

You can check if your division is correct by using another kind of math—multiplication. Multiplication and division are connected to each other. Multiplying 20 by 4 makes 80, which is the total number of flyers I started with.

> Multiplication and division work together.
> If I know $20 \times 4 = 80$, then I also know $80 \div 4 = 20$.

80 ÷ 4 = 20

20 × 4 = 80

SCHOOL ELECTION

LOPEZ FOR PRESIDENT!

Besides flyers, I have buttons and pencils to give to the students who are voting. I have a box of buttons and pencils. There's an equal number of both. How can I find out how many total objects are in the box?

I know that the box holds 2 equal groups of objects. I count 25 pencils. I don't even need to count the buttons. All I have to do is think of what number makes 25 when it's divided in half, or by 2. It's 50, so the box has 50 total objects.

The buttons and pencils have my name on them. When the students in my class use them, they'll remember to vote for me!

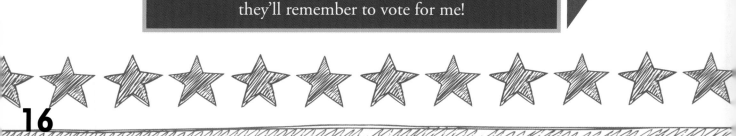

$? \div 2 = 25$ $50 \div 2 = 25$

Time to Vote

Soon, the class election is here. I'm very nervous, but I did a good job campaigning. I hope everyone votes for me! The students in my class use a **ballot** to vote for the person they want to be president.

There are 24 kids in my class, and they sit at 4 tables. There's an equal number of students at each table. How many ballots should my teacher give to each table?

This equation is easy. Divide the total number of students by the number of tables to find the answer.

I ran against 2 other students who also wanted to be president, so the students in our class have 3 people to choose from. They pick the person they think will do the best job.

I have to get more votes than the others in order to win. A tie happens if we all get the same number of votes. What number of votes would we each need in order to make a tie? Use division to find out.

Divide 24, the total number of votes, by the number of students running for president, which is 3. That gives you the number of votes that would result in a tie.

$$24 \div 3 = ?$$

Vote for President

And the Winner Is...

My teacher counts the votes. Luckily, there isn't a tie! I won because I got more votes than the other 2 students. I'm happy I won, but it's important to be nice to the people who lost. They worked just as hard as I did.

I'm excited to be the class president. I have a lot of good ideas that will make this school year really fun. I can't wait to get started!

Glossary

ballot (BAA-luht) A piece of paper used to record someone's vote.

campaign (kam-PAYN) To actively work to win votes; also, everything done to win votes in an election.

divide (duh-VYD) To split something into equal shares.

flyer (FLY-uhr) A paper telling people about something.

represent (reh-prih-ZEHNT) To act for others.

Index

Due to the changing nature of Internet links, The Rosen Publishing Group, Inc., has developed an online list of websites related to the subject of this book. This site is updated regularly. Please use this link to access the list: www.powerkidslinks.com/mm/oat/elec